Why.

The three natural laws and the four personal choices that explain why the world is the way it is.

John B. Moore

ISBN-10: 1530103525

ISBN-13: 978-1530103522

Dedication

To all persons who believe that democracy and
common sense result in the best government.

*"The more sand that has escaped from the hourglass of our life, the
clearer we should see through it."*: Jean Paul

Contents

Preface

This is a book about *why* the world is the way it is and the immutable forces that determine its future. It is not about the physical aspects of our world such as the environment or the impact of technology but rather describes the cause-and-effect relationships that determine how individuals, organizations and societies behave -- thus the title "*Why.*" The book does not advocate specific behavior – it is not normative – but rather presents an explanation of why the world exists as it is.

Why has three main parts. Part 1 has two chapters. Chapter 1: *Three Natural Laws* describes three universal truths. Chapter 2: *Four Choices That Govern Our Behavior* describes four choices that we make implicitly or explicitly that influence our actions. In Part 2, separate chapters focus on Career Choices, Management, Government and Unions. In each case, we ask if the actions are in accordance with the three Natural Laws and how the decisions made reveal belief in each of the four behavioral choices. Part 3 — The Future of Western Societies, explains why societies in the West are in decline and what can be done to make the world a better place for the next generation.

Enjoy.

Numerous statements in this book are general in nature and claimed as factual. As with all generalizations, some readers will disagree strongly with the assertions because exceptions exist. When numeric values are present, I have done my best to get supporting data from articles and reports published on the web. Please let me know of significant mistakes via Facebook (JB Moore) or email (jbmsavvy@gmail.com). I apologize in advance for any errors.

J.B.Moore, March 2016

Part 1: Laws and Choices

Laws and Choices presents the basis for the assertions, opinions and arguments that follow in Parts 2 & 3.

Chapter 1 defines three cause-effect relationships that exist independently of actions of individuals or organizations.

Chapter 2 defines four criteria that individuals use when making decisions that have a moral or ethical aspect. These four beliefs are also associated with decisions made by organizations.

Chapter 1: The Three Natural Laws

"We may brave human laws, but we cannot resist natural ones.": Jules Verne

Wikipedia defines a law as *"a statement of fact, deduced from observation, to the effect that a particular natural or scientific phenomenon always occurs if certain conditions are present"*.

It is in this sense that this Chapter describes three universal truths that are beyond the control of any individual or group. These are:

- The Law of Supply and Demand
- Survival of the Fittest
- Life Has No Guarantees

#1 The Law of Supply & Demand

"Supply and demand is perhaps one of the most fundamental concepts of economics and it is the backbone of a market economy": Reem Heaka

Everyone has an intuitive understanding of "the law of supply and demand". A simple instance is "if you really want something, you are willing to pay a higher price for it." More formally, the law of supply and demand describes the relationship among: the demand for something, the supply (availability) of that something, and the price which people will pay for that something. Because there are three entities involved -- demand, supply and price, it is difficult to show the interaction of these factors on a two dimensional chart. There are really two parts: The law of Supply says the supply (availability of a good or service) increases with the price buyers are willing to pay. For example, if consumers are willing to pay big bucks for a smart phone, the number of high-priced cell phone choices will increase. This relationship is shown in the graph below.

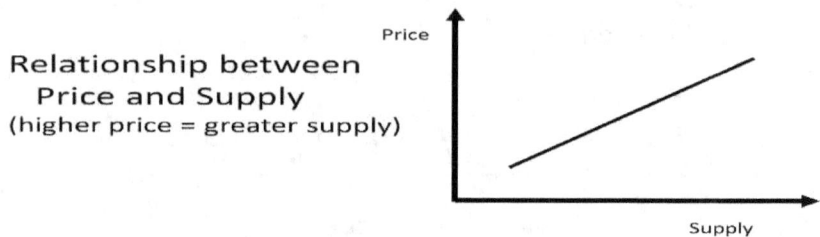

Relationship between
Price and Supply
(higher price = greater supply)

The second part – the law of demand – says that the demand for a good or service decreases with an increase in the price. For example, if the price of cauliflower goes up, we eat less cauliflower. This is shown graphically below.

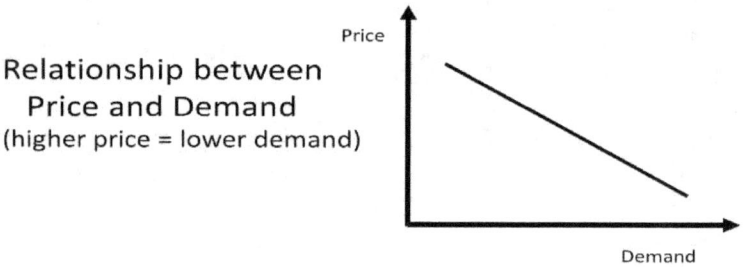

Relationship between
Price and Demand
(higher price = lower demand)

We all understand these laws intuitively. What is the price that balances supply and demand? A good example occurs during a typical auction. That is for a given item being auctioned, the equilibrium (balancing) price is the selling price. That is there is no demand at a higher price. When the supply curve is overlaid on the demand curve, the point where the lines cross defines the price and quantity that balances supply and demand.

The quantitative nature of these relationships and how they are affected by inflation, taxation and other factors is the subject matter of every introductory course in Economics.

Natural Law #1 is *"The Law of Supply and Demand cannot be superseded by the actions of an individual, organization or society"*. The truth of this law can however be used to advantage by manipulating the demand (e.g. via advertising) or controlling the supply (e.g. withdrawing services) or price fixing. However, actions such as these are proof of the universal belief in its validity. More will be said in the chapters dealing with government and unions.

#2 The Law of Survival of the Fittest

> *"Survival of the fittest is commonly used today to refer to a supposed greater probability that 'fit' as opposed to 'unfit' individuals will survive some test."*: Wikipedia

> *"Survivors aren't always the strongest; sometimes they're the smartest, but more often simply the luckiest."*: Carrie Ryan

> *"There's no such things as survival of the fittest. Survival of the most adequate, maybe. It doesn't matter whether a solution is optimal. All that matters is whether it beats the alternative."*: Peter Watts

The notion of luck is linked to *probability* found in the Wikipedia statement. *Luck* by definition is transient in nature and therefore lucky survival is not permanent. One could paraphrase Ryan's statement to suggest that those that are *always* lucky survive. This assertion is however discounted in Natural Law #3 in the next section. Peter Watts' statement includes the idea of an optimal solution. This implies that survival is the optimal solution. However, there is no concept of optimality in survival since that would imply "to die is to fail". To survive is to survive.

An example. Millions of years ago, dinosaurs were among the most fit animals on the earth. So why didn't they survive? The impact of a giant asteroid or comet off the coast of Central America 66 million years ago released dense clouds of dust that blocked the sun's rays, darkening and chilling Earth to deadly levels for most plants and, in turn, many animals. When the dust finally settled, greenhouse gases created by the impact caused temperatures to skyrocket above pre-impact levels. Scientists believe that these frigid and sweltering climatic extremes caused the extinction of not just the dinosaurs, but of up to 70 percent of all plants and animals living at the time. Many species of insects did survive however because they were the most adaptable.

Let's be clear. We are not talking about fitness being physical fitness or mental fitness or emotional fitness or spiritual fitness or economic fitness or legal fitness but rather the ability to adapt. Thus a paraphrase of Law #2 is *"The Most Adaptable Survive"*.

#3 Life Has No Guarantees

> *"God not only plays dice, but also sometimes throws them where they cannot be seen.":* Stephen Hawking

> *"The post office doesn't guarantee delivery, but it tries really hard. It's called best-efforts communication. If you put two postcards in the post-box, they don't necessarily come out then in the same order that you put them in. So, that means that there's potentially disorder with your delivery, and that's also true in the Internet.":* Vint Cerf

> *"As long as you have capital punishment there is no guarantee that innocent people won't be put to death.":* Paul Simon

A guarantee is a promise or assurance that certain conditions will be fulfilled or certain future events will or will not occur. A typical commercial guarantee is something like "we offer a 10 year guarantee against rusting". A key element of a guarantee is the notion of "certainty" even when it includes a probabilistic condition such as "within 2 percent 19 times out of 20". In cases such as this, the "2 percent" and "19 times out of 20" are used to imply certainty.

Guarantees encompass product guarantees, service guarantees, satisfaction guarantees, money-back guarantees and the business of insurance – i.e. a promise of specific results should specific events occur. The whole world of contract law revolves around guarantees of behavior of the contracting parties.

The assertion in Law #3 is that no one has the ability to predict the future with certainty. No one can predict when the big earthquake will hit the West coast of North America or whether you will get hit by a vehicle when crossing the street or if you will be present when a terrorist attack occurs. Of course we can make any prediction more precise by adding probability to the statement as in "There is a 40% chance of precipitation today." However, the accuracy of that statement cannot be tested until time passes and thus it is not a guarantee. We should not confuse accuracy or precision with certainty.

In theory, if one knew all the laws that govern the behavior of all elements of the universe, then one could create an algorithm that given the current state of the universe, would be able to calculate all future states of the universe with certainty – thus providing a guarantee of the future. The existence of such a hypothetical capability is subject to the paradox that the algorithm would be able to predict the results of its own calculations before doing the calculations – it would be an algorithmic selfie. If such a thing were possible, there would be no need for algorithms!

Natural Law #3 is "No individual or group has the ability to guarantee anything in the future" -- except, paradoxically, the truth of this law.

Chapter 2: Four Choices That Govern Our Behavior

This chapter describes four choices that individuals make either explicitly or implicitly that govern how they behave. After observing another person's behavior, you may be able to infer what choices the decision-maker's actions implied. To avoid making these four choices/beliefs true-false assertions one could add the phrase "under the following conditions" or "but this is where I draw the line". That however would open the door to endless dialog. The intent is simply to identify four mutually exclusive beliefs or filters that humans apply when making decisions that have an ethical aspect. Expressed as statements the four choices are:

- Every other person is as important to his/her self as you are to your self
- I am my brother's keeper
- The end justifies the means
- My brother is my keeper

#1 Other People are as Important to Themselves as You Are To Your Self

> *"I have no right, by anything I do or say, to demean a human being in his own eyes. What matters is not what I think of him; it is what he thinks of himself. To undermine a man's self-respect is a sin.":* Antoine de Saint-Exupery

This may sound like the traditional Golden Rule that has been expressed in many different ways such as "Do unto others as you would have them do unto you." The difference here, however, is that a statement such as "Do unto ..." is normative – telling us what we *should* do. However, the statement #1 above is not a command but only that we *make a choice* about the relative worth or importance of other persons. It simply says we may choose to believe that all mortals are equal or not.

Many celebrities, politicians and others certainly view themselves as more important than others. This belief is used to justify their actions in many situations. No doubt the Russian President considers himself more important than a typical Russian peasant. A pedophile, aside from satisfying hormonal needs, ignores any self-importance the victim feels. Corruption and cheating at all levels does not consider the self-worth of those affected. Choice #1 says if you put yourself "In the other guy's shoes" is their self-importance equal to your own? We make choices about the empathy we have or don't have for our fellow human beings.

#2 I Am My Brother's Keeper

> *"If a free society cannot help the many who are poor, it cannot save the few who are rich.":* John F. Kennedy

Do you believe you are responsible for others' welfare? What degree of altruism do you have? Clearly, the statement "I am my brother's keeper" is one that most people would append "up to a point". Nonetheless, many people are at one end or other of the altruism scale. Persons range from being willing to sacrifice one's life for that of a total stranger to "every man for himself". Most of us are somewhere in the middle and make case-by-case choices regarding charitable actions.

A middle-of-the-road dilemma occurs in choices related to health care. Would you contribute a dollar a week to provide an indigent person with a life-sustaining drug? How about ten dollars a week? How about a thousand dollars as week? Should the government pay one-hundred-thousand dollars to keep someone alive for one more day? Clearly we draw the line at different points but the choice is conscious and is reflected in our behavior.

The person who believes "an eye for an eye" does not believe in being "my brother's keeper". It is someone who believes that the penalty should match the crime. They believe that individuals are responsible and accountable for consequences of their own behavior. In their mind, this absolves them from being their brother's keeper.

#3 The End Justifies the Means

"The end may justify the means as long as there is something that justifies the end.": Leon Trotsky

"The first sign of corruption in a society that is still alive is that the end justifies the means.": Georges Bernanos

Does the achievement of an objective justify the means used to attain the objective? In the 9/11 crisis, Vice President Cheney, when informed that there could be more hijacked planes in the air beyond the two that had flown into the World Trade towers, had to decide whether to shoot down these planes carrying many innocent civilians or let them fly into other buildings which might kill people in the planes and those in the targeted buildings. What would you do?

Some choices have small consequences. An example is lying to your child about Santa Claus while still preaching "always be honest". Others choices are much more consequential such as a decision to go to war or to drop a nuclear bomb.

Some believe that rights and wrongs of actions should be judged in terms of the consequences that follow. If there are two possible outcomes, choose the one that produces more happiness, reduces more suffering, provides greater freedom, or some other "good" result. Others however believe that we have a duty to do *the right thing* regardless of the consequences. This is a fundamental principle of most religions – God wants me do to this to eliminate evil. This is used as justification for doing bad in order to do right.

We choose whether or not the end justifies the means thousands of times in our lifetime.

#4 My Brother Is My Keeper

> *"The consuming desire of most human beings is deliberately to plant their whole life in the hands of some other person. I would describe this method of searching for happiness as immature. Development of character consists solely in moving toward self-sufficiency.":* **Quentin Crisp**

Some people believe the world owes them a living. They believe that if they are in trouble, you are obligated to come to their aid. Others believe that each of us is responsible for our own welfare – that we have no right to reach into someone else's pocket or conscience to solve our problems.

This choice is the flip side of "I am my brother's keeper". Furthermore, one can be extremely charitable and at the same time not expect charity from anyone else. On the other hand, one can expect others to look after all their needs but feel no compulsion to help others.

We all know people who believe and demand that the government (or others) should guarantee them employment, food to eat, free healthcare, etc. Other people view the largesse of other persons or organizations as a bonus and not an obligation.

"Is my brother my keeper?" is a choice we all make and like the three previous choices manifests itself in our personality and actions.

Summary

Decisions that include a moral or ethical aspect reflect our answers to four implicit or explicit questions. Although we may judge the actions of others based on our own answers to these questions, the purpose of this discourse is simply to suggest that these questions go a long way toward explaining the 'why' of people's behavior.

Many actions manifest multiple beliefs. For example, a statement such as "Win at all Costs." spans more than one choice. In particular, it implies assigning unequal respect for the opposing parties; it implies that the negative consequences of losing are not the responsibility of the victor; and it implies that the end justifies the means.

The next Part of this monograph explains how the Three Natural Laws and the Four Behavioral Choices reveal themselves in personal and public actions.

Part 2: Laws and Choices Revealed

"The universal order and the personal order are nothing but different expressions and manifestations of a common underlying principle.": Marcus Aurelius

The following chapters explain how the Three Natural Laws and Four Behavioral Beliefs are revealed and manifested by the actions of people and organizations in four different contexts. In each case, two questions are posed:

- Do the actions of the individual or group obey the Three Natural Laws?
- What do the decisions and actions reveal about each of the behavioral beliefs?

The chapters focus on:

- Career choices
- Management
- Government
- Unions

Chapter 3: Career Choices

"When I look at acting careers that I really admire, I see that it's been a precise decision-making process for these people. They make decisions based on what they love, and they do only the things that they are passionate about. They play only characters that they can't stop thinking about.": Taylor Swift

In my twenties I was confronted with the choice of what to do with my life. Instead of waiting for happenstance to make the choice I asked the question "For people that I admire, what is the focus of their life that has given them purpose and satisfaction?" This analysis led to identifying four distinct choices. These are (the pursuit of):

- Knowledge
- Wealth
- Power
- Service

This is not to suggest that any one of these is better than any other -- only that these categories represent relatively distinct career choices.

The table below suggests how these choices reflect the personal beliefs described in Chapter 2. A dash indicates the belief is not a major factor.

Belief	Knowledge	Wealth	Power	Service
Other person's self-importance equals mine	-	-	-	-
I am my brother's keeper	No	No	Yes	Yes
The end justifies the means	No	No	Yes	-
My brother is my keeper	Yes	Yes	-	-

Of course, many people choose a combination of the four career choices but often one dominates. Furthermore, the yes/no values in the table may be the opposite for some people. For example, some may seek wealth as a means of helping the poor. Nonetheless the choice made by most individuals falls into one of knowledge, wealth, power or service.

My own choice was to devote my energies to pursue each of these goals sequentially but be ready to stick with one of them if it provided self-fulfillment.

Career choices are also influenced by the three Natural Laws. The law of supply and demand is often an important factor in choosing a career. If the demand for software engineers is much larger than that for civil engineers, enrolment in software engineering courses will increase. If there is a surplus of elementary school teachers looking for work in a region, prospective teachers will look farther afield. If baseball players get paid more than hockey players, the supply of baseball hopefuls will become relatively greater.

Survival of the fittest is also a factor. Some individuals welcome competition and are confident they will rise up the corporate ladder or bureaucratic hierarchy. Others look for employment with limited responsibilities.

Guarantees are important to some people. Employment that includes defined-benefit pensions, healthcare plans and loyalty bonuses is often a determining factor when job hunting.

Perhaps some people were "born to be a _____". Most of us could find fulfillment in many different careers. As Yogi Berra said "When you come to a fork in the road, take it."

Chapter 4: Management

"Good management is the art of making problems so interesting and their solutions so constructive that everyone wants to get to work and deal with them.": Paul Hawken

Management can be defined in many ways. Common to all definitions is the idea that management involves the organization and coordination of the activities of an entity in order to achieve one or more objectives. Managers perform tasks that encompass the following functions: forecasting, planning, organizing, commanding, coordinating and controlling. Each of these can be a challenge to define precisely. Of these the most difficult is the meaning of "control". In the author's view the best metaphor describing control is "keeping the bubble between the lines". The bubble metaphor relates to is the one found in a carpenter's level to determine whether an object is perfectly horizontal or vertical. Control in this sense involves monitoring, diagnosing, prescribing/proscribing and taking actions to achieve an objective.

Managers have wide ranges of competence and many different styles. The relevance to this Chapter is that the actions of any particular manager reflect his or her four personal choices or beliefs. Pick any manager you know and assign him/her a yes or no for each of the four choices. Do their actions indicate that they: view everyone as equals? Are they altruistic? Do their results justify the methods used to achieve objectives? Do they accept responsibility for the consequences of their decisions?

The responsibility choice is – in the author's view – one that is essential to principles of good management. Managers must delegate tasks (otherwise they wouldn't be managers!). The principle is *"responsibility if and only if accountability"*. The two terms are often confused but shouldn't be. Responsibility implies authority to take action. Accountability is attributing success or failure to an individual or group following an action. Responsibility is the cause producing the effect; accountability is culpability or credit for failure or success. The principle states that if someone has responsibility, they must also be accountable AND that if a person is accountable, they must have been given the responsibility.

It is truly amazing in large bureaucracies in particular how often this principle is ignored. We have all had experiences where no one wants to make a decision (they might be responsible or accountable) or, if responsible, they are ready to point the finger of blame at someone else. How often have war criminals said "I was only following orders"? or "my mother made me do it." or "I did not make that decision." Consider the result when a child gets access to a parent's firearm with tragic results. In this case, who is responsible? Who is accountable? In general, using mental illness as a defense in a murder trial makes separating responsibility and accountability very difficult. President Truman's statement *"The buck stops here"* demonstrated his willingness to be accountable without having direct responsibility for many decisions made without his direct involvement.

In summary, managers' decisions demonstrate the degree of belief they have in each of the four assertions of personal behavior.

Do managers act in accordance with the three Natural Laws? For example, does a manager's decision to hire a relative obey the law of supply and demand? Are promised rewards for good performance always realized? Mangers whose actions always obey the three Natural Laws are seldom found.

Chapter 5: Government

"Government's first duty is to protect the people, not run their lives.": Ronald Reagan

"Be thankful we're not getting all the government we're paying for.": **Will Rogers**

This Chapter is the lengthiest in the book. It summarizes the role of government and asks if government actions obey or contradict the natural laws of: supply and demand; survival of the fittest; and life has no guarantees. This is followed by commentary on whether a government's decisions parallel the choices made by its constituents. The attempt is to be non-judgmental, and simply to tell it like it is.

The Role of Government
How would you define the role of government at an arbitrary level – national, regional or local? Wikipedia defines government as *"the system by which a **state** or community is controlled".* Of course, different levels of government have different responsibilities but there are common elements in all. The most important role involves management (see previous Chapter) of a wide scope of resources – financial, persons and organizations to name three, and responsibility for defining and modifying rules of governance of all activities within its sphere of responsibility.

Governments acquire and maintain control of their responsibilities in different ways, the most common being democratic, fascist, military power and dictatorship. Regardless of the method of control, governments evince degrees of belief in the four choices made by individuals.

The functions performed by governments are management functions but what motivates the decisions that are made? This is discussed in greater detail in the section "Government and the Four Behavioral Choices". However, most people in Western societies would concur that governments should provide services for its constituents that:

- Enable them to achieve personal goals through public education, health care and financial support
- Protect them from unwanted actions by their neighbors
- Protect them from unwanted actions by other governments

In the following section, we address the question of whether the actions of governments obey the Three Natural Laws and in the subsequent section we ask if violations of the Natural Laws can be explained by the four Behavioral Beliefs that can be inferred from government actions.

Government and the Three Natural Laws

First, let us examine whether government actions comply with the Three Natural Laws. Readers may disagree with the statements made in this subsection but those objections likely correlate with whether or not government's actions align with the Behavioral Beliefs of its citizens.

#1 The Law of Supply and Demand.

Recognizing the power of the law of supply and demand is the fundamental premise of free enterprise societies and open markets. Commercial products and businesses succeed or fail based on their ability to provide goods and services at prices buyers are willing to pay. On the supply side, success or failure is also a consequence of good decision-making regarding the cost of acquiring the resources necessary to run a business.

Do governments "go with" the law of supply and demand? Or, do they act to manipulate and control the supply and/or demand for products and services? Most everything a government does is an attempt to suppress the law of supply and demand. Examples abound. In financial management, the whole purpose of tariffs, subsidies, tax exemptions and credits is to manipulate the law of supply and demand. Minimum wage laws are a direct contradiction of the law of supply and demand unless the legislated wage level should happen to reflect the true equilibrium price of supply and demand for labor. An extreme example of supply control is paying people NOT to grow agricultural products.

On the supply side, national governments have a unique power – control of the money supply. They do this through printing money, unlimited borrowing power and/or incursion of deficits. Clearly we want governments to use this power wisely. A country in which everyone is given a printing press to balance their personal supply and demand for money is absurd but it is fun to consider the hypothetical consequences. Although governments are generally not a primary producer of goods, governments use other mechanisms to control supply. For many government contracts, there is a list of approved suppliers. There are restrictions on corporate mergers and takeovers. There are licensing requirements and thousands of regulations and user fees designed to control both the supply of and demand for goods and services.

#2 Survival of the Fittest

Do governments act to promote survival of the fittest? Definitely not. In fact, most people living in democracies view an important role of government as that of assisting those who are less fit or at-risk economically, health-wise, legally, educationally and/or other conditions of human existence. For example, if governments practiced survival of the fittest, there would be no bailouts of businesses that would otherwise fail. Financial, healthcare and educational resources would be directed to organizations and individuals who would need the least help in order to survive and thrive. This would be done in order to create a country or region that was wealthier, healthier and smarter. There would be a greater proportion of elite citizens (the weak would fall by the wayside) which presumably would make the country more fit when competing with other nations or regions. The Nazi regime is a good example of a government that went to extreme lengths to create a society dominated by an elite race.

Why governments do not act to promote survival of the fittest is discussed in the subsection "Government and the Four Behavioral Choices".

#3 Life Has No Guarantees

Natural Law #3 states that events occur beyond the control of any person or organization. Government promises however do not reflect belief in this law – they are replete with guarantees. There are guarantees for health care, for income security, for safe food, for a good education, for fire and police protection, for efficient and corrupt-free government services and a myriad of other societal benefits. Of course, none of these can be "guaranteed". When a promise is not fulfilled, the governments acknowledge the truth of Law #3 with a phrases such as "Times have changed; it was beyond our control; we could not have foreseen ..."

Of course, not all promises/guarantees fail. Many come true and unanticipated events may produce positive results that increase the promised benefits.

Politicians rely on the public's gullibility to believe that guarantees are equivalent to certainty. Because life has no guarantees, they should really be called intentions.

Government and the Four Behavioral Choices
Having argued that government actions consistently violate the Three Natural Laws, the question is, can government actions be rationalized based on the four beliefs evinced by those actions? Paradoxically, the question is "does the end justify the means?" Consider each of the four beliefs.

Belief #1: All people are equally important.

This belief is supported by government actions that give the electorate equal entitlement to government services. However, many would argue that these entitlements are not equally distributed to all persons; that governments demonstrate favoritism to individuals and groups who are recipients of government largesse; that there are political payoffs in the form of sinecures and contracts to those who support government policies and election efforts.

Governments always profess belief in equality but it is not always practiced.

Belief #2: I am My Brother's Keeper

Western societies have greatly increased their degree of public altruism in the last hundred years. Clearly, in democratic countries, the electorate has increasingly supported public welfare as opposed to relying solely on the personal altruism and charitable actions of its citizens. Cynics would argue that public welfare lets private citizens claim they are being their brother's keeper via tax-supported government programs.

There are tremendous numbers of private initiatives to help disadvantaged individuals and groups. When international catastrophes occur involving famine, floods, refugees, many people provide aid beyond that provided by governments. Governments encourage and often reward this behavior by matching private donations with public funds.

Because democratic governments are elected by the will of the majority, the degree to which governments act as their brother's keeper usually reflects the personal beliefs of its subjects.

Belief #3: The End Justifies the Means

We have argued in a preceding section, government actions contravene the laws of Supply & Demand, Survival of the Fittest, and Life has no Guarantees. Nonetheless, many view that government actions are justified by belief in the two principles of equality and altruism discussed in previous paragraphs. The big question is "Are actions which do not obey the Three Natural Laws sustainable?" This is the primary focus of Part 3 of this book – "The Future of Western Societies".

Aside from the challenging question of sustainability, governments have the authority to decide if war is justified; if torture is justified; if any or all of abortions, assisted suicide and the death penalty can be justified. Already a vigorous debate has begun on whether human genetic engineering is acceptable. All of these questions lie within the government's sphere of responsibility and require answering the question "Does the end justify the means?".

Belief #4. My Brother Is My Keeper

There are two separate issues. The first is "Does a government believe that the public has this belief?". Equivalently, do government actions suggest that individuals and organizations are accountable for their own actions? There is evidence on both sides of this question.

On the "not accountable" side is the belief in "I am my brother's keeper" – regardless of the behavior of an individual or group. Thus, governments act to provide support to persons and organizations whose problems were caused by poor choices or bad luck. An example is the provision of quality healthcare and treatment for addicted smokers, alcoholics and gamblers. Corporate bailouts that reward poor business decisions and pensions for those who chose not to save for the future is another.

On the "make the bed you lie in" side, governments certainly draw the line in many instances. For example, few individuals are rescued from personal bankruptcy; people in remote communities do not receive the same level of services as residents in large municipalities; hospitals have committees that may deny life-continuation treatments to those in need.

The second issue is whether governments believe that the public is *its* keeper. The answer has two parts. First, governments have the power to raise taxes, charge fees and pass regulations that allow it to remain in power. Implementation of these actions implies that the government believes that the electorate is responsible for being the government's keeper. Second, in democracies, government powers are renewed or withdrawn at defined intervals. Elections therefore answer the question of a government's belief that the public is its keeper.

Chapter 6: Unions

"My problem with unions is they breed mediocrity": Kevin
O'Leary

Many organizations are created to provide economic benefits to its members. Unions, trade associations, marketing boards, self-regulated professions and employee associations are examples. Of these, unions are perhaps the most prevalent. Unions were created to oppose the "divide and conquer" strategy used by corporations to suppress (control the supply of) employee benefits. In a free society, freedom of association is deemed a right and unions have produced major improvements in the quality of working conditions for union members.

In this Chapter the word "union" is used as a surrogate for any well-defined organized group of workers.

Before discussing unions in some depth, it should be said that marketing boards – lumber, grain, milk and poultry are examples – are generally overt in stating that their raison d'être is supply management. Primarily through production quotas, these organizations attempt to control the supply and price of their products. This is done "in order to have a stable and orderly market". Professional associations on the other hand, typically use fee schedules and licensing requirements as a means of affecting the equilibrium point of supply and demand.

Unions have many parallels to governments in terms of the functions they perform in order to achieve member benefits. They have constitutions, elections, bureaucratic hierarchies, programs and projects designed to achieve union objectives. As with governments, one can ask whether union actions are contrary to the Three Natural Laws and to what extent their decisions indicate their belief in each of the four Behavioral Beliefs described in Chapter 2.

With respect to the three Natural Laws, the most important is compatibility with the law of supply and demand. The power of a union arises from its ability to withdraw the supply of labor provided to one or more organizations. By withdrawing labor, the union attempts to motivate the employer to raise the price of labor to a level that is mutually agreeable. If no agreement is reached, then in theory, union members will seek other employment and the employer will hire new employees. In practice, this seldom happens. Reasons follow.

First, there are many laws that grant unions rights and privileges. Some of these pertain to rights of union members to opt in or opt out of membership. More important is the right to prevent an employer from using non-employees to perform union work during a strike. This use of so-called scab labor that denies others the right to work is essentially a control on labor supply. Morally, whether this is right or wrong relates in some ways to each of the four behavioral beliefs held by the union.

A second issue related to supply and demand occurs when a union has a monopoly on the services it supplies. This monopolistic situation is most frequently associated with unions that provide government services. Examples are teachers' unions, police, firefighter and paramedic unions, civil servant unions and healthcare workers' unions. In the private sector, exclusivity of supply also occurs. For example, unions in the entertainment industry may have contracts that require the employer to use only union workers. However, in the private sector, the employer has a choice to renew or not renew the contract with the same union. In the public sector, this is not the case because the union has a monopoly on the supply of services.

When negotiating the financial terms of employment contracts, an effective strategy used by labor groups that have a monopoly on supplying services is to muddy the distinction between "benefit" and "value". The word "benefit" means something of advantage to a person or group. What may be a benefit to some, may be disadvantagous to others. The word "value" on the other hand implies that a unit of measurement – often monetary -- of an advantage can be associated with a benefit. Values can be positive or negative. When developing business strategies, a cost-benefit analysis is often performed to estimate the net value of an action or decision. Currently, the term "business case" has supplanted "cost-benefit analysis" as the label for the method of determining the net profitability of a strategy.

In labor negotiations with management, the labor side typically threatens loss of public benefits rather than loss of value if labor services are withdrawn. Police, firefighters and healthcare workers for example, emphasize the loss of benefits (not value) to the public if their demands are not met. By increasing the FUD (fear, uncertainty and doubt) factor, they attempt to increase public support for their position.

Two questions that need to be answered are:

- What public benefits are increased by acceding to the labor group's demands?
- What is the increased cost of the hypothetical incremental benefits to the public?

For example, how does the public benefit by providing paternity leave to a government employee? Or, how does the payment of a loyalty bonus to a firefighter improve the level of fire protection? In examples such as these, the employee receives a positive value whereas the public value is negative.

In summary, it makes sense to receive improved service and benefits *from* publically-supported workers but we should always ask if we are getting good value.

With respect to the four behavioral beliefs, union choices are made to support the purpose of the union. Thus: union members are more important than others; the "brother" in my brother's keeper is a union member; actions are justified if they help achieve the objectives of the union; and "my brother is my keeper" becomes "my union is my keeper".

In summary, unions can provide their members with significant benefits. The legal rights of unions have evolved well beyond a means of balancing supply and demand and have augmented the power of unions to effectively control the supply of labor to a greater or lesser degree. For unions in the public sector that have a monopoly on the supply of workers, balancing supply and demand would require removing the right to strike and allowing the employer to contract out work to others.

Part 3: The Future of Western Societies

"The future ain't what it used to be.": Yogi Berra

What does it all mean? Can one forecast the future of human societies using compliance with the three Natural Laws and manifestations of the four Behavioral Beliefs as the means of predicting the future? Unlike the statements made in Parts 1 and 2 which were presented as being factual, the content in Part 3 deals with predictions. Thus, Natural Law #3 applies – no guarantees.

Underlying the discussion which follows is the requirement for *purpose*. That is, one may be able to predict the future to some extent, but is the forecasted state of society better or worse than the current state. In this monograph, the predictions relate to the quality of life in Western societies. Much more will be said in the following two chapters.

Chapter 7: Western Societies, a SWOT Analysis

When planning for the future, many organizations perform a SWOT (Strengths, Weaknesses, Opportunities, Threats) analysis as a framework for organizing relevant factors and ideas. Two of these attributes – Strengths and Weaknesses – are internal with respect to the organization. Opportunities and Threats on the other hand involve factors that may be beneficial or harmful to achieving the organization's objectives but which are external to the organization's environment. The table below summarizes this structure.

SWOT Analysis

	Helpful	Harmful
Internal	Strengths	Weaknesses
External	Opportunities	Threats

External Opportunities and Threats

Threats
There are two classes of threats – global threats to all societies, and threats specific to Western societies. First, global threats. The list below was compiled by the *Oxford Future of Humanity Institute*.

- Nuclear War
- Artificial intelligence, Humanoid robots
- Synthetic life forms (synthetic DNA, designed humans)
- Nanotechnology (Tiny machines designed to 'live' inside human bodies)
- Global system collapse

- Global pandemic
- Super volcano
- Major asteroid impact
- Ecological catastrophe
- Extreme climate change
- As yet unknown risks (no guarantees!)

The first five items result from technological developments and, as with all advances in technology, the technology can be used for good or evil – guns for example. Technology creates both opportunities and threats.

> *"We cannot quite know what will happen if a machine exceeds our own intelligence, so we can't know if we'll be infinitely helped by it, or ignored by it and sidelined, or conceivably destroyed by it."*: Rollo Carpenter

> *"The challenge is to eat the fruit without the worm."*: Julian Savulescu

Threats from non-Western societies include:

- Military advantages resulting from superior weaponry and strategies
- Economic threats caused by high productivity and trading prowess
- Terrorism initiatives

Opportunities

Aside from opportunities arising from advances in technology, economic opportunities for Western societies exist because:

- Western societies have internal strengths (see next subsection)
- The world is a global marketplace
- Consumerism (the theory that it is good for people to spend money on goods and services) is growing
- Online retailing is feasible and efficient
- Rapid, long distant movement of supplies and finished goods is relatively inexpensive

Regarding the last bullet, it is interesting that the technology associated with air travel enables us to *move* 150 times faster than walking but computers enable us to *compute* billions of times faster than the speed of our cognitive processes.

Highly profitable opportunities in the global market place may be difficult to identify and challenging to exploit. Long-term return on investments cannot be realized without obeying the Three Natural Laws.

Internal Strengths

In general, what are the strengths of Western societies? They encompass the following:

- Stable, democratic governments
- Well-educated, large populations
- Significant natural resources
- Widespread use of modern technology
- Wealth that provides a large pool of investment capital
- Rewards for inventions and innovations that spawn successful businesses

These internal strengths enhance the probability of success when exploiting both internal and external opportunities. These factors have resulted in Western societies having the highest standards of living in the world.

Internal Weaknesses

A major thesis of this dialectic is that the quality of life in Western societies is declining because of internal weaknesses. A surrogate for this conclusion is found in the answer to the question "Are today's children better off or worse off than their parents?" Not all Western societies have the same weaknesses. Much has been written about the decline of America. See for example the article in the July 2015 issue of *Fortune* that lists twelve factors that support this assertion. Among these are the facts that: median wealth per adult is the <u>worst</u> of 27 high income countries; child poverty in the U.S. ranks 34th out of 35 countries; and that America has the highest prison population in the world.

All societies that have achieved a dominant position over large numbers of people have had power that, over time, involved phases of ascendancy, dominance and decline. This was true for the ancient Egyptian society, the Chinese Dynasties, the Mayan civilization, the Roman and Ottoman Empires and others. In the twentieth century Western societies have had a strong, widespread influence on events, economies and global culture. Where is The West in the lifecycle of societal domination?

Externally, Western societies have achieved their dominant position by exploiting military, economic and technological advantages. Advanced weaponry and tactics were significant factors in winning two World Wars. Economic dominance had its seeds in the industrial revolution by taking advantage of greatly increased productivity resulting from use of inventions and innovations such as the steam engine, the cotton mill and the assembly line. More recently, the United States was the first country to develop and recognize the commercial potential of computational power and digital communications in creating products for global markets.

If one accepts the foregoing arguments and also that Western societies show no obvious decrease in their desire to maintain their advantage in factors contributing to dominance, is there any reason to believe that

Western societies will lose their preeminent position? The answer is "yes". There are two causes of this decline – external and internal.

External causes were listed in the "Threats" subsection above. To reiterate some of these points, a non-Western society could become more "fit" than Western societies and become dominant by:

- Winning a war by deploying nuclear weapons
- Massive terrorist attacks including biological warfare
- Exploiting technology advantages in artificial intelligence and/or genetic engineering
- Supplying material and labor resources at substantially lower costs

It is the author's belief that although external forces *may* result in the further decline of Western societies, that the decline of the West is, and will continue to be, caused by internal factors.

Internal Causes of Decline. There are four main causes:

- The imbalance between private and public sector enterprise
- Levels of public sector compensation
- Increasing government deficits and debt
- Weaknesses in public education

For each of these causes, the relationship between the cause and the three Natural Laws and the four Behavioral Beliefs is explained.

Weakness #1: Private/Public Sector Imbalance

There is indisputable evidence that the public share of domestic GDPs is growing in all Western democracies. The evidence includes facts that public sector salaries and benefits are rising faster than private sector compensation; that the total tax rate is increasing faster than the cost of living; that the so-called "tax freedom day" is becoming later each year; and that the percentage of people employed in the public sector continues to increase.

Taken in isolation, one might say of public sector employees – "lucky for them" but the consequences are dire. The desirable balance between public and private enterprise is like a teeter-totter. That is, to work well, each side needs to contribute to the other's success and enjoyment which can only be done if the load is balanced. If one side gets too heavy, the other side can't keep their feet on the ground to fulfil their purpose. Continuing the metaphor, this works both ways. If the private sector is up in the air, it can't support the public sector and push the economy forward; if the public sector is too light, necessary public services are not performed. A balance is needed.

Although the following illustration is over-simplistic, the underlying premise has validity. Suppose the tax rate for individuals and corporations is 20%. Then for each new person being funded by tax dollars, one needs five private sector taxpayers to pay for the public sector worker. Although the public sector worker returns 20% of his/her remuneration to the public treasury, this is more than offset by the transfer of a tax-paying private sector worker to a tax-consuming public sector employee thus further reducing the ratio of private-to-public-sector workers. Where is the tipping point? At what point does the growth in the public sector become unsustainable? Once exceeded, the only method of sustainable solvency is socialism – government ownership of the means of production. Some would argue that this is desirable. Others would argue that the relatively limited degree of socialism (or State control) in Western societies has made them the fittest to survive.

Weakness #2: Levels of Public Sector Compensation

> *"A government that robs Peter to pay Paul can always depend on the support of Paul.":* George Bernard Shaw

> *"It's OK to want to feather one's own nest but there should be a law that prevents using the other guy's feathers":* J.B.Moore

According to a study conducted by *the Canadian Federation of*

Independent Business, federal employees, versus those in the private sector, receive "a salary premium of 13 per cent, which swells to 33.2 per cent when you factor in benefits".

Presumably, employees are rewarded for the value they contribute – the higher the value, the greater the reward. With material goods, selling price is assumed to reflect value; however, with intangible attributes such as one's carbon footprint, value is much more difficult to measure. In this subsection a distinction is made between the "value case" and the "business case" criteria for determining fair compensation for employees.

Consider, for example, the European Union which has 55,000 bureaucrats that work in the European Commission, Council, Parliament and Court of Justice. The increase in employees between 2000 and 2010 at the Council was 52.5% and in the Parliament 90.8%. The average pay raise commitment for 2016 is 2.4% (well above the cost of inflation) and is being back-dated six months. The average middle management salary is about $150,000 and the tax rate is 13.4%. All of this may be reasonable if the value added by these employees is justified.

The primary output of this bureaucracy is a seemingly endless number of bans, prohibitions, restrictions, regulations and edicts being enacted by unelected bureaucrats. These enactments are claimed as necessary to improve the energy efficiency, environmental friendliness and health standards of the EU members. The resulting improvements comprise the societal *benefits* added by the bureaucrats. Critics however claim that the majority of these controls have a negative *value*. For example: What *value* is added by only allowing cucumbers a bend of 10mm per 10cm of length? Or, according to a 60-page technical report on European toilets and urinals—which took two years and an undisclosed amount of public money to complete—EU experts have decided to set the average flush volume as "the arithmetic average of one full flush volume and three reduced flush volumes." What is the incremental *value* added to society by this pronouncement? What value could have been added by alternative deployment of the resources used?

The EU has taken the role of a whipping boy in the preceding paragraph but similar, questionable value-added premises can be found in all Western democracies. Consider now the business case which asks if the costs are justified.

The business case involves assessing productivity and net benefits. In spite of the questionable benefits/values illustrated by the preceding examples, many government services are absolutely necessary and do provide real benefits to the electorate. How does the productivity of the delivery of government services compare with the productivity of the private sector? (The production of goods by governments is ignored since almost all government outputs are services.) Productivity is essentially the ratio of outputs to inputs which this case is the ratio of the value of the services to the cost of providing the services. If government services were contracted out to the private sector – and many are -- would the productivity ratio increase or decrease? A large component of cost is the payroll cost. In the private sector, owners' performance is tied to profits which – ceteris paribus – can be increased by reducing costs. Thus private sector employers are motivated to pay only what is necessary to deliver acceptable product quality and/or an acceptable level of service. This is not the case with the departments that deliver government services because there is no profit incentive. The consequence is that the cost of supplying government services exceeds that determined by the law of supply and demand.

Overpaying employees makes it easier to acquire a large pool of applicants and thus mitigates the risk of hiring a poor performer. As evidence of this fact, consider that every year in the European Union between 25,000 and 30,000 people apply for a job as a civil bureaucrat. At the end of the competition, roughly 100 are employed. The supply of applicants far exceeds the need/demand for employees. This high ratio of applicants to job openings is found in practically all government jurisdictions and is a clear indication that the cost of public sector workers is higher than necessary.

A second example. In the author's home town, city hall staff requested the addition of three new positions with publically-posted suggested salaries. To the writer, the salaries seemed excessive and would result in a huge number of applications. What would happen if the suggested salaries were cut in half? Would no qualified applicants apply? Clearly the compensation levels should be set to attract a reasonable number of qualified applicants and the resulting cost savings should benefit the taxpayers. Hypothetically, if public sector salaries were reduced by one-third, how many employees would resign? How many of those who resigned would find work in the private sector at their previous salary? The results of such a survey would be enlightening.

Of course, the private sector has many perceived instances of overpaid employees. Professional sport is one area where salaries seem uncorrelated with common values. A good major league pitcher's salary of $16,000,000 per season works out to a payment of five thousand dollars per pitch – good or bad. The differences of course are that player salaries do obey the law of supply and demand and secondly, the public is not responsible for poor roster decisions.

We have all heard the phrase "too big to fail". This economic theory asserts that certain corporations and institutions are so large that their failure would be disastrous to the national or regional economy and therefore they must be supported by government when facing potential failure. There have been successes and failures resulting from government bailouts.

Does the opposite theory "too big to succeed" apply to government bureaucracies which have been growing faster than private sector employment in the last fifteen years? Government laws and regulations are designed to control and restrict individual and corporate behavior to protect us from ourselves and/or from each other. (What was the last regulation that actually increased individual freedom?) Given that humans are basically tribal, and as such, advocate and practice tribal behaviors that differ widely, it is impossible for any large, centrist authority to regulate citizens' actions in a way that is acceptable to all tribes. The government's strategy to solve this problem is to pass legislation and issue regulations that often includes hundreds of "earmarks" or exemptions. Paradoxically, the process of negotiating and modifying laws and regulations requires expanding the level of bureaucratic participation thus further increasing the imbalance between public and private employment.

In summary, one of the major weaknesses of Western societies is that actions by governments and their associated large bureaucracies contravene the law of supply and demand for employees by offering compensation packages that are more generous than necessary to provide the public benefits derived from these services. This has two negative consequences. First, it necessitates higher taxes and therefore reduces the private sector's productivity because of higher costs. The effect is to give external organizations competitive advantages.

Weakness #3: Public Sector Deficits and Debt

> *"A national debt, if it is not excessive, will be to us a national blessing."*: Alexander Hamilton

> *"When you're in a hole, stop digging"*: Denis Healey

It took the U.S. federal government 200 years to produce its first $1 trillion budget. Washington now runs annual deficits twice as large and U.S. federal unfunded liabilities exceed $88 trillion. The Province of Ontario has the largest sub-national per capita debt in the world.

Economists have written much about the issue of whether public debt has a significant negative effect on a country's economic growth. When the debt is expressed as a percentage of GDP, there is a fairly strong consensus that negative effects begin around 70% and become significant growth depressors above 90%. If one examines this ratio for a list of countries, it is clear that the "have not" countries are at risk. The disturbing fact however is that this percentage is increasing in the "have" countries as well. Governments are aware that there is increasing pressure from the public to balance revenues and expenses. Political parties seeking office show awareness of the electorate's concern by typically guaranteeing/promising that, if elected, the books will be balanced right *after* their term of office has expired.

Governments can reduce the debt burden by either paying down the debt or by reducing deficits. Ways of increasing revenues include:

- Expanding the monetary supply
- Borrowing
- Increasing taxation
- Increasing user fees
- Selling assets
- Voodoo economics and accounting

Because increasing taxes has such an obvious effect on citizens' disposable incomes, most government opt for a combination of other revenue-generating strategies. To satisfy the insatiable demand for more revenue, there has been an explosion in government user fees, license fees, permit fees, levies, tolls, and utility charges. This allows politicians to claim they are "holding the line" on tax increases when in fact the total claim on private sector funds has increased significantly.

The city adjacent to the writer's home town has over 1600 different user fees. Most of the resulting revenue is used to cover the cost of administering the collection of the fees meaning that this is a very inefficient method of increasing net revenue.

Deficit reduction can be achieved in many ways. Reducing payroll costs described as Weakness #2 above is only one. Other ways of reducing expenses include:

- Reducing services
- Reducing transfer payments to subordinate public entities
- Reducing payments to non-government persons
- Scaling down commitments for promised projects and programs

Each of these has a political cost which makes it difficult to implement.

Often the phrase "we owe it to ourselves" is used as an attempt to reduce public concerns about the ever-escalating public debt. In the United States, approximately 113 trillion dollars is owed to bond holders – half of whom are foreigners who expect to be paid back. If it can't be paid back through resulting increases in taxes and user fees, then let's call it what it is – the cost of being my brother's keeper and/or fostering the attitude that "the public is my keeper". Otherwise it's just voodoo economics.

In the author's view, for the foreseeable future, public deficits and debt will continue to increase, thus further weakening Western societies. Political candidates are very good at instilling a "free lunch" mindset in voters. They convince voters that increased services and benefits can be provided without increasing the cost to the individual voter.

Weakness #4: Weaknesses in Public Education

> *"The whole purpose of education is to turn mirrors into windows"*: Sydney J. Harris

> *"If American schooling is inadequate now, just imagine how much more obsolete it will be when today's kindergarten students graduate from high school in just 12 years"*: Janet Napolitano

Every society allocates resources for compulsory education of children. In the long term, the required participation by students, the subject matter, forms of instruction, qualifications for teachers and expected outcomes reflect the will of the people. There is no single agreed-upon measure of the quality of education – it is multi-dimensional.

In Western societies – the U.S. in particular – there is ample evidence of the dumbing down of public education. On the website infowars.com, see for example the test for 1912 Eighth Grade students in spelling, arithmetic, grammar, geography, physiology, civil government, and history. Would you pass that test?

Not only is the amount of knowledge acquired by students decreasing but the motivation to perform well is being eroded. Some evidence: an Edmonton high school teacher (Lynden Dorval) was suspended for giving students zeros on uncompleted assignments or exams; last year the York Region District School Board failed only six 8th Grade students out of 8000+; when questioned, a student said "If students show up they deserve a minimum mark. A zero seems a bit extreme."

> *"Winners are not afraid of losing. But losers are. Failure is part of the process of success. People who avoid failure also avoid success."*: Robert T. Kiyosaki

Research has shown that if you want to develop kids' self-esteem, the best way to do it is to praise everything they do and make excuses for their failures. But if you want to develop their character, you do almost the opposite: You let them fail and don't hide their failures from them or from anybody else – not to make them feel lousy about themselves, but to give them the tools to succeed next time.

Some educational theorists suggest more emphasis should be placed on the behavioral aspects of education. Instead of focusing on acquiring knowledge, they espouse the metaphor of one world-sized schoolhouse where the focus is compassion, engagement and citizenship. They endorse the message in Robert Fulghum's marvelous poem *"Everything I Need to Know I Learned in Kindergarten"*. However, should that be the primary outcome of public education?

Does the use of technology benefit those who take online courses or who participate in computer-based learning in classroom settings? Many research studies have been completed and the results are not conclusive. The biggest advantage of computer-based instruction is that for a given learning target the time can be variable – i.e. learning at the student's pace. This contrasts with the lock-step --fixed time, variable amount learned – traditional approach. Research has further revealed the importance of social interaction among students in achieving learning success. Technology cannot yet match the benefits of face-to-face interactions but it is only a matter of time until advances in virtual reality mitigate this differentiator.

Are teachers leading the charge to improve our educational systems? There certainly are many thousands of dedicated, highly-skilled teachers who embrace means and methods that improve the productivity of the teaching profession and its contributions to society. On the opposite side are the threats of automation and union policies.

Regarding technology, Michael Saylor said *"The hallmark of any good technology is that it destroys jobs."* Teaching jobs are not exempt. Given the financial constraints faced by school boards, there will be increasing public pressure to replace significant numbers of teachers with advanced technologies. This development will be strongly opposed by teachers unions which have unique advantages. They have virtually no competition; they can operate as inefficiently as they want and never go bankrupt; they are masters at resisting accountability and entrenching rigid work rules that protect their members; they don't have to worry that their employer will go out of business; teachers are popular; there are so many of them; and, teacher strikes are an awful nuisance to many people.

In summary, the weaknesses of our public educational systems contribute to the demise of Western societies because:

- Students today have relatively much less knowledge than in the past
- Students are shielded from the benefits of failure
- Benefits from good uses of technology are not being realized
- Teachers unions self-interests have priority over improvements in education

Collectively, these weaknesses make Western societies less fit to survive in the competitive global economy of the 21st Century.

Chapter 8: Preventing the Decline of Western Societies

"The system that enables the most people to earn the most success is free enterprise, by matching up people's skills, interests, and abilities. In contrast, redistribution simply spreads money around. Even worse, it attenuates the ability to earn success by perverting economic incentives": Arthur C. Brooks

"The problem with socialism is that you eventually run out of other peoples' money.": Margaret Thatcher

The Problem

Before making the mistake of running around with a solution looking for a problem, let's make sure we satisfy the five requirements necessary to have a well-defined problem. These are that there must be:

- a person or group that "has" the problem
- a state that is deemed more desirable than the status quo
- a choice of one or more actions that are available to the owner of the problem
- a finite probability that each candidate action will produce the desired outcome
- a state of doubt as to which is the best choice

It is assumed that for the problem we are trying to solve: 1) the owner of the problem is a Western society; 2) the desired state is a society in which the children have a better quality of life than their parents; 3) the choices are actions which will reduce the weaknesses in current societies; 4) the proposed actions do not contravene any of the three Natural Laws and are compatible with the Four Behavioral Choices of the majority of persons in the society; 5) there is no current consensus on what to do.

The problem as presented above is very abstract and hence an analogous surrogate problem will be used to make the proposed principles of a good solution clearer.

A Pie Analogy

Suppose that all persons must get their food from a single pie. The problem is choosing what recipe to use, how big to make it, and how to slice the pie so that everyone gets a fair share. The pie represents the economy. The ingredients are the human, financial and other resources used to produce the goods and services that constitute the resulting pie. The recipe specifies the amount of each ingredient to use and instructions for combining them. The size of the pie must be sufficient to feed all the people who are entitled to be fed.

For our economic pie, persons who are members of the society are entitled to be fed. The recipe must specify the fractions of public and private employment and the source and allowed uses of financial resources. The pie must be protected from being stolen or poisoned by persons who are not being fed.

There are many potential recipes for making a satisfactory pie. However, the one chosen must be such that:

- The price paid for the ingredients must be at fair market value (the equilibrium point of supply and demand)
- The size of the pie and the nutritional value of the ingredients must be sufficient to keep the consumers in good health (survival of the fittest)
- The recipe may need to change if unexpected or uncontrollable events occur (life has no guarantees)

There will be people who contribute a lot of the ingredients and effort to make the pie; some will make no contributions and most will contribute something as well as receiving a slice of the pie. Some contributors will provide kitchen security while others will do research to create better recipes.

Although the size of each person's slice should be decided by the majority of all those entitled to be fed, it is expected that slice sizes will reflect:

- the contributions made by each person and
- the minimum amount of food that non-contributors should receive (I am my brother's keeper) and
- the methods used to determine the recipe and the size of slices (the end justifies the means) and
- the demands of non-contributors for a bigger slice (my brother is my keeper)

That the size of a pie-maker's slice should be correlated with (but not solely determined by) contributions is an assumption which is generally acceptable in a society founded on free enterprise principles.

So, what should the recipe be? Each of us would choose a different recipe and it's unlikely that any two people would have the same rules for slicing the pie. Everyone should contribute to the discussion of the recipe and the size of the slices. The recipe and allocation rules that are chosen should be selected from competing proposals and be acceptable to the majority.

There is no perfect recipe and no allocation policy that will seem fair to everyone but that is why democracy is the fairest form of government. Winston Churchill said *"It has been said that democracy is the worst form of government except all the others that have been tried"*. Those who espouse the principles of socialism in which government owns the means of production and distribution may disagree with the Churchill's pronouncement.

The motivation for this monograph has not been to recommend a specific recipe and its rules of entitlement but simply to state the principles that must apply in order to have a better pie than the one we now have.

Chapter 9: Summary

The primary objective of this book has been to explain why the world is the way it is.

Part 1 contains two major propositions:

- There are three universal truths (Natural Laws) that cannot be changed by individuals or organizations. These are:
    - The Law of Supply and Demand: the underlying force driving economic activity
    - Survival of the Fittest: an argument that adaptability is an absolute requirement for survival
    - Life Has No Guarantees: the impossibility of predicting the future with certainty
- There are four beliefs or behavioral choices made by individuals and organizations that determine the decisions and actions. These are:
    - Other people are as important to themselves as you are to your self
    - I am my brother's keeper
    - The end justifies the means
    - My brother is my keeper

Part 2 asks if individuals and organizations act in accordance with the three Natural Laws and how their decisions reveal their Beliefs and Behavioral Choices. Separate chapters focus on Career Choices, Management, Governments and Unions.

Part 3 of the book discusses the future of Western societies by analyzing the strengths and weaknesses of these societies. Evidence shows that the quality of life in the West is declining. The last chapter uses a pie-making analogy to define the principles that could create a society that reverses the decline. The fundamental principle is that regardless of the recipe chosen, the pie-makers must obey the three Natural Laws and that the rules of entitlement for a fair slice should reflect the majority's belief in each of the four Behavioral Choices.

Appendix

The following parable was published by the Canadian Federation of Independent Business.

The Little Red Rooster

Once upon a time there was a Little Red Rooster who scratched about and uncovered some grains of wheat. He called his barnyard neighbors and said "If we work together and plant this wheat, we will have some fine bread to eat. Who will help me plant the wheat?"

"Not I", said the Cow. "Not I", said the Duck. "Not I", said the Goose. "Then I will" said the Little Red Rooster and he did.

After the wheat started growing, the ground turned dry and there was no rain in sight. "Who will help me water the wheat?" said the Little Red Rooster. "Not I", said the Cow. " I'd lose my workers compensation" said the Pig. "Not I", said the Duck. "Equal rights", said the Goose. "Then I will", said the Little Red Rooster and he did.

The wheat grew tall and ripened into golden grain. "Who will help me reap the wheat?" asked the Little Red Rooster. "I'm waiting for a guaranteed annual wage" said the Cow. "Not I" said the Duck. "Out of my classification" said the Pig. "Not I" said the Goose. "The I will", said the Little Red Rooster and he did.

When it came time to grind the flour, "Not I" said the Cow. "I'd lose my unemployment insurance" said the Duck.

When it came time to bake the bread. "That's overtime for me" said the Cow. "I'm a dropout and never learned how" said the Duck. "I'd lose my welfare benefits" said the Pig. "If I'm the only one helping, that's discrimination" said the Goose. "Then I will" said the Little Red Rooster and he did. He baked five loaves of fine bread and held them up for his neighbors to see. "I want some" said the Cow. "I want some" said the Cow. "I want some" said the Duck. "I want some" said the Pig. "I demand my share" said the Goose. "No" said the Little Red Rooster. "I will rest for a while and eat them myself". "Excess profits" cried the Cow. "Capitalist leach" screamed the Duck. "Company Fink" screamed the Goose. And they hurriedly planted picket signs and marched around the Little Red Rooster singing "We Shall Overcome." And they did.

When the Farmer came to investigate the commotion, he said "You must not be greedy, Little Red Rooster. Look at the oppressed Cow. Look at the disadvantaged Duck. Look at the underprivileged Pig. Look at the less fortunate Goose. You are guilty of making them second-class citizens". "But-but-but I earned the bread" said the Little Red Rooster.

"Exactly," the wise Farmer said. "That is the wonderful free enterprise system; anybody in the barnyard can earn as much as he wants. You should be very happy to have all this freedom. In other barnyards, you would have to give all your loaves to the Farmer. Here you give four loaves to your suffering neighbors."

And they lived happily ever after. Including the Little Red Rooster who smiled and crowed "I am grateful. I am grateful." But his neighbors wondered why he never baked any more bread.

ABOUT THE AUTHOR

Dr. John B. Moore's career has included being a secondary school teacher, computer systems engineer with IBM, professor of Management Sciences at the University of Waterloo, professional speaker, software developer, consultant, businessman and author. He has many varied interests that involve technology, sports, music, bridge and community service. He resides in Waterloo, Ontario with his wife of many years.

www.ingramcontent.com/pod-product-compliance
Lightning Source LLC
Chambersburg PA
CBHW071251280526
45788CB00004B/1672